Last One Picked

Written by Jenny Feely
Illustrated by Pat Reynolds

sundance

I love playing basketball. At my old school, I was best in my class.

Everyone in my new class loves basketball, too. We play basketball every recess, every day.

Joe owns the basketball. So, he always gets to be a team captain. His best friend, Tony, always gets to be the other team captain.

Until today, I was always the last one picked.

3

Today, I looked for a way
to show them I could play.

Like every other day,
I lined up with everyone
who wanted to play.

4

"I'll pick first," said Joe.

"Pick me," I said.

"I'll take Jack," said Joe.

"I pick Mario," said Tony.

"Me! Me! Pick me next!" I said.
"I can run fast. Pick me."

"Anna," said Joe.

"Frank," said Tony.

"Wang," said Joe.

"I'm a good shot," I said. "Pick me!"

"I pick Jan," said Tony.

"Let's play," said Joe.

"Joe!" I yelled.
"What about me?"

"What?" said Joe.

"Please!" I said. "Please let me play!"

"OK," said Joe. "You can play
on Tony's team."

9

We started to play.

Tony got the ball and threw it to Jan. She scored a basket.

Joe got the ball and scored a basket. Then Jan had the ball again.

"Throw it to me!" I yelled.

Jan threw the ball to Mario.

We played and played.
No one threw the ball to me.

"The score is tied," said Joe.
"The next basket wins."

I ran down the court and waited.

Joe ran down the court with the ball.
He didn't think I could stop him.

Before he knew what was happening,
I grabbed the ball from him.
My teammates cheered.

"Here! Here!" yelled Mario.
"Throw it to me!" yelled Jan.
"Go for it!" yelled Tony.

I stopped. I looked at the basket.
I shot the ball.

Everyone stood and watched.
No one said anything.
The ball went up and up and up.

Whoosh!

The ball swished right through the net.

"Yea!" yelled everyone. "That was great! We didn't know you could play!"

"Thanks for the chance," I said to Tony.

"I bet you don't get picked last anymore," Tony said with a grin.